Study to Shew Thyself Approved

Bible Scriptures for Everyday Living

C J Barber

ISBN:
9798711977155

Table of Contents

Section 1: Introduction

These Bible verses are references for when you need guidance concerning everyday living. If you read through these scriptures repeatedly, they could literally change your life, if you let them. Many years ago I remember having to learn different Bible scriptures for Bible Study Class. In fact, they were written down for us in a little notebook form to keep in our pocket. They were always with us for reference.

"STUDY TO SHEW THYSELF APPROVED", gives a breakdown of where to find those various scriptures for whatever is going on in your life and to bring you closer to God. Use God's Word as a guide in your lives no matter what you may be going through.

This book is no replacement for the Bible. It is just a fraction of what you will find in the Bible. We need to brush up on these verses, especially during this time. Keep this booklet with you.

The scripture verses in this book are from the King James Version, NIV and the AMP versions of the Bible.

I hope these will help you as much as they have helped me.

May God Richly Bless You

Section 2: Types of Love

We know that God is love. The ancient Greek had four words to show the difference between the various forms of love. Agape, Eros, Philia & Storge. Below you will see the seven different forms and intensities of each type of love:

Agape is Universal, Unconditional love. Jesus showed this type of love when He died on the cross for our sins. *John 3:16*

Eros is Romantic love. It is the intimate love between husband and wife. (*The word Eros will not be found in the New Testament. However, this type of love is definitely shown in the Old Testament, the Song of Solomon.)*

Philia is Friendship or Affectionate love. How a Christian should feel towards one another.

Storge (pronounced: STOR-*jay)* is Familiar love. Such as love between parents and children and between brothers and sisters. (*Even though the actual word Storge does not appear in the Bible)*

Pragma is Enduring love. The everlasting love between a couple that has been together for a long time has Pragma love.

Philautia is Self-Love or Self-Compassion. A form of Philautia love is caring for one's self. An example of this love is by eating healthy, exercising, going to the doctor's office when necessary, and taking medication as prescribed.

Ludas is a Playful type of love. Such as flirting, seduction, and sexual behavior.

Section 3: Love Scriptures

We learned of the seven types of love described in the Bible. However, there are over 100 Bible verses speaking of love. We are only going to view a fraction of those verses.

<u>1 John 4: 8 NIV</u>

Whoever does not love does not know God, because God is love.

<u>Psalms 143:8 NIV</u>

Let the morning bring me word of your unfailing love, for I have put my trust in you.

<u>I Corinthians 13:1-5 (NIV)</u>

If I speak in the tongues of men or of angels, but do not have love, I am only a resounding gong or a clanging cymbal. (2) If I have the gift of prophecy and can fathom all mysteries and all knowledge, and if I have a faith that can move mountains, but do not have love, I am nothing. (3) If I give all I possess to the poor and give over my body to hardship that I may boast, but do not have love, I gain nothing. (4) Love is patient, love is kind. It does not envy, it does not boast, it is not proud. (5) It does not dishonor others, it is not self-seeking, it is not easily angered, it keeps no record of wrongs.

<u>I Corinthians 13:13 NIV</u>

And now these three remain: faith, hope and love. But the greatest of these is love.

Luke 10:27

And he answering said, Thou shalt love the Lord thy God with all thy heart, and with all thy soul, and with all thy strength, and with all thy mind; and thy neighbor as thyself.

John 14:15

If ye love me, keep my commandments.

Colossians 3:14 NIV

And over all these virtues put on love, which binds them all together in perfect unity.

1 John 3:16

Hereby perceive we the love of God, because he laid down his life for us: and we ought to lay down our lives for the brethren.

Matthew 3:17

And lo a voice from heaven, saying, This is my beloved Son, in whom I am well pleased.

1 Peter 4:8 NIV

Above all, love each other deeply, because love covers over a multitude of sins.

Lamentations 3:22-23 NIV

Because of the Lord's great love we are not consumed, for his compassions never fail. (23) They are new every morning; great is your faithfulness.

Luke 6:35

But love ye your enemies, and do good, and lend, hoping for nothing again; and your reward shall be great, and ye shall be the children of the Highest: for he is kind unto the unthankful and to the evil.

John 15:12

This is my commandment, That ye love one another, as I have loved you.

Romans 8:28

And we know that all things work together for good to them that love God, to them who are the called according to his purpose.

John 13:34-35

A new commandment I give unto you, That ye love one another; as I have loved you, that ye also love one another. (35) By this shall all men know that ye are my disciples, if ye have love one to another.

Ephesians 5:25-26 NIV

Husbands, love your wives, just as Christ loved the church and gave himself up for her (26) to make her holy, cleansing her by the washing with water through the word,

I John 4:20

If a man say, I love God, and hateth his brother, he is a liar; for he that loveth not his brother whom he hath seen, how can he love God whom he hath not seen?

Romans 12:9 NIV

Love must be sincere. Hate what is evil; cling to what is good.

Proverbs 3:3-4 NIV

Let love and faithfulness never leave you; bind them around your neck, write them on the tablet of your heart. (4) Then you will win favor and a good name in the sight of God and man.

I Corinthians 2:9

But as it is written, eye hath not seen, nor ear heard, neither have entered into the hearts of man, the things which God hath prepared for them that love him.

Song of Solomon 8:6 NIV

Place me like a seal over your heart, like a seal on your arm; for love is as strong as death, its jealousy unyielding as the grave. It burns like a mighty flame.

I John 4:19

We love him, because he first loved us.

Psalms 116:1-2

I love the Lord, because he hath heard my voice and my supplications. (2) Because he hath inclined his ear unto me, therefore will I call upon him as long as I live.

Mark 12:30

And thou shalt love the Lord thy God with all thy heart, and with all thy soul, and with all thy mind, and with all thy strength: this is the first commandment.

Section 3.1: Your Notes on Love
We learned of the seven types of love and the many scriptures concerning love. List the ones you need to improve on and name the scripture that explains why.

Section 4: Scriptures on Faith

How strong is your faith? If you pray, but you really don't believe that God will answer your prayers. Then why did you pray. Let's see what God says about faith.

Hebrews 11:1

Now faith is the substance of things hoped for, the evidence of things not seen.

Hebrews 11:6

But without faith it is impossible to please him: for he that cometh to God must believe that he is, and that he is a rewarder of them that diligently seek him.

Matthew 17:20 NIV

He replied, "Because you have so little faith. Truly I tell you, if you have faith as small as a mustard seed, you can say to this mountain, 'Move from here to there,' and it will move. Nothing will be impossible for you."

Romans 10:17

So faith cometh by hearing, and hearing by the word of God.

Matthew 21:22

And all things, whatsoever ye shall ask in prayer, believing, ye shall receive.

I John 5:5

Who is it that overcomes the world? Only the one who believes that Jesus is the Son of God.

John 8:24

"I said therefore unto you, that ye shall die in your sins: for if ye believe not that I am he, ye shall die in your sins.

Ephesians 2:8-9

For by grace are ye saved through faith; and that not of yourselves: it is the gift of God: (9) Not of works, lest any man should boast.

Mark 9:23

Jesus said unto him, "if thou canst believe, all things are possible to him that believeth."

Mark 11:24

"Therefore I say unto you, what things soever ye desire, when ye pray, believe that ye receive them, and ye shall have them.

John 20:29

Jesus saith unto him, Thomas, because thou hast seen me, thou hast believed: blessed are they that have not seen, and yet have believed.

Ephesians 3:16-17

That he would grant you, according to the riches of his glory, to be strengthened with might by his Spirit in the inner man; (17) That Christ may dwell in your hearts by faith; that ye, being rooted and grounded in love,

Proverbs 3:5-6

Trust in the Lord with all thine heart; and lean not to thy own understanding. (6) In all thy ways acknowledge him, and he shall direct thy paths.

James 1:2-4 NIV

Consider it pure joy my brothers and sisters, whenever you face trails of many kinds, (3) because you know that the testing of your faith produces perseverance. (4) Let perseverance finish its work so that you may be mature and complete, not lacking anything.

James 1:5-6 NIV

If any of you lack wisdom, you should ask God, who gives generously to all without finding fault, and it will be given to you. (6) But when you ask, you must believe and not doubt, because the one who doubts is like a wave of the sea, blown and tossed by the wind.

John 6:35

And Jesus said unto them, I am the bread of life: he that cometh to me shall never hunger; and he that believeth on me shall never thirst,

Galatians 2:16 NIV

Know that a person is not justified by the works of the law, but by faith in Jesus Christ. So we, too, have put our faith in Christ Jesus that we may be justified by faith in Christ and not by the works of the law, because by the works of the law no one will be justified.

Philippians 4:13

I can do all things through Christ which strengtheneth me.

Matthew 15:28

Then Jesus answered and said unto her, O woman, great is thy faith: be it unto thee even as thou wilt. And her daughter was made whole from that very hour.

Romans 8:31

What shall we then say to these things? If God be for us, who can be against us?

Matthew 14:30-31 NIV

But when he saw the wind, he was afraid and, beginning to sink, cried out, "Lord, save me!" (31) Immediately Jesus reached out his hand and caught him. "You of little faith," he said, "why did you doubt?"

I Corinthians 2:3-5 NIV

I came to you in weakness with great fear and trembling. (4) My message and my preaching were not with wise and persuasive words, but with a demonstration of the Spirit's power, (5) so that your faith might not rest on human wisdom, but on God's power.

. 2 Corinthians 5:7

For we walk by faith, not by sight

Mark 10:51-52

And Jesus answered and said unto him, " What wilt thou that I should do unto thee?" The blind man said unto him, Lord, that I might receive my sight. (52) And Jesus said unto him, "Go thy way; thy faith hath made thee whole." And immediately he received his sight, and followed Jesus in the way.

James 2:14-17 NIV

What good is it, my brothers and sisters, if someone claims to have faith but has no deeds? Can such faith save them? (15) Suppose a brother or a sister is without clothes and daily food. (16) If one of you says to them, "Go in peace; keep warm and well fed," but does nothing about their physical needs, what good is it? (17) In the same way, faith by itself, if it is not accompanied by action, is dead.

James 2:18 NIV

But someone will say, "You have faith; I have deeds." Show me your faith without deeds, and I will show you my faith by my deeds.

Mark 5:36

As soon as Jesus heard the word that was spoken, he saith unto the ruler of the synagogue, "Be not afraid, only believe."

Section 4.1: *Your Notes on Faith*

After reviewing the various scriptures on faith, write down the specific ones that is helping you with your faith walk.

Section 5: Scriptures on Comfort

During one time or another in our lives, we all have gone thru disappointments and sadness. These few Bible verses are just a sample of how God's Word could comfort you if you would let Him.

Psalms 46:1

God is our refuge and strength, a very present help in trouble.

Psalms 18:2

The Lord is my rock, and my fortress, and my deliverer; my God, my strength, in whom I will trust; my buckler, and the horn of my salvation, and my high tower.

Psalms 55:22

Cast thy burden upon the Lord, and he shall sustain thee: he shall never suffer the righteous to be moved.

Psalms 37:24

Though he fall, he shall not be utterly cast down: for the Lord upholdeth him with his hand.

Nahum 1:7

The Lord is good, a stronghold in the day of trouble; and he knoweth them that trust in him.

John 16:33

These things I have spoken unto you, that in me ye might have peace.   In the world ye shall have tribulation: but be of good cheer; I have overcome the world.

Matthew 11:28

Come unto me, all ye that labor and are heavy laden, and I will give you rest.

Matthew 5:4

Blessed are they that mourn; for they shall be comforted.

Psalms 27:14

Wait on the Lord; be of good courage, and he shall strengthen thine heart: wait, I say, on the Lord.

Psalms 138:7

Though I walk in the midst of trouble, thou wilt revive me: thou shalt stretch forth thine hand against the wrath of mine enemies, and thy right hand shall save me.

Psalms 34:19

Many are the afflictions of the righteous; but the Lord delivered him out of them all.

Psalms 22:24 (NIV)

For he has not despised or scorned the suffering of the afflicted one; he has not hidden his face from him; but has listened to his cry for help.

Psalms 9:9

The Lord also will be a refuge for the oppressed, a refuge in times of trouble.

Psalms 30:5

For his anger endureth but a moment, in his favor is life: weeping may endure for a night, but joy cometh in the morning.

Psalms 119:76

Let, I pray thee, thy merciful kindness be for my comfort, according to thy word unto thy servant.

II Corinthians 1:3-4 NIV

Praise be to the God and Father of our Lord Jesus Christ, the Father of compassion and the God of all comfort, (4) who comforts us in all our troubles, so that we can comfort those in any trouble with the comfort we ourselves receive from God.

Matthew 25:36

I needed clothes and you clothed me, I was sick and you looked after me, I was in prison and you came to visit me.

Matthew 25:37-39

Then the righteous will answer him, "Lord, when did we see you hungry and feed you, or thirsty and give you something to drink? (38) When did we see you a stranger and invite you in, or needing clothes and clothe you? (39) When did we see you sick or in prison and go to visit you?"

Matthew 25:40

The King will reply, Truly I tell you, whatever you did for one of the least of these brothers and sisters of mine, you did for me.

Romans 12:3

For I say, through the grace given unto me, to every man that is among you, not to think of himself more highly than he ought to think; but to think soberly, according as God hath dealt to every man the measure of faith.

Matthew 10:29-31NIV

Are not two sparrows sold for a penny? Yet not one of them will fall to the ground outside your Father's care. (30) And even the very hairs on your head are all numbered. (31) So don't be afraid; you are worth more than many sparrows.

I John 1:9

If we confess our sins, he is faithful and just to forgive us our sins, and cleanse us from all unrighteousness.

Deuteronomy 31:8 NIV

The Lord himself goes before you and will be with you; he will never leave you nor forsake you. Do not be afraid; do not be discouraged.

John 16:22 NIV

So with you: Now is your time of grief, but I will see you again and you will rejoice, and no one will take away your joy.

Romans 12:15 NIV

Rejoice with those who rejoice; mourn with those who mourn. (16) Live in harmony with one another. Do not be proud, but be willing to associate with people of low position. Do not be conceited.

Psalms 86:17 NIV

Give me a sign of your goodness, that my enemies may see it and be put to shame, for you, Lord, have helped me and comforted me

II Thessalonians 3:3 NIV

But the Lord is faithfull, and he will strengthen you and protect you from the evil one.

Jeremiah 31:3

The Lord hath appeared of old unto me, saying, yea, I have loved thee with an everlasting love: therefore with lovingkindness have I drawn thee.

Lamentations 3:60-61 NIV

You have see the depth of their vengeance, all their plots against me. (61) Lord, you have heard their insults, all their plots against me.

Romans 12:19

Dearly beloved, avenge not yourselves, but rather give place unto wrath: for it is written, "Vengeance is mine; I will repay," saith the Lord.

Section 5.1: *Your Notes on Comfort*

After reviewing the few Bible verses concerning comfort, list in your own words how God will comfort you.

Section 6: Scriptures about Fear

The year 2020 has been a crazy year to remember. The worldwide pandemic, unemployment, violence, death, and financial problems just touch on a few fears. A reality that we all had to experience one way or another. . What shall we do? Throughout the Bible, it tells us to pray without ceasing. The following scriptures are just a few concerning fear. Read them out loud and let them soak in. Incorporate them in your prayers and remember God is in control.

Mark 4:40

And he said unto them, why are ye so fearful? How is it that ye have no faith?

II Timothy 1:7

For God hath not given us the spirit of fear; but of power, and of love, and of a sound mind.

John 14:27

Peace I leave with you, my peace I give unto you: not as the world giveth, give I unto you. Let not your heart be troubled, neither let it be afraid.

Proverbs 3:24

When thou liest down, thou shalt not be afraid: yea, thou shalt lie down, and thy sleep shall be sweet.

Hebrews 13:6

So that we may boldly say, The Lord is my helper, and I will not fear what man shall do unto me.

Proverbs 29:25

The fear of man bringeth a snare: but whoso putteth his trust in the Lord shall be safe.

Psalms 23:4

Yea, though I walk through the valley of the shadow of death, I will fear no evil: for thou art with me; thy rod and thy staff they comfort me.

Psalms 112:1

Praise ye the Lord. Blessed is the man that feareth the Lord, that delighteth greatly in his commandments.

Philippians 4:6-7

Be careful for nothing; but in everything by prayer and supplication with thanksgiving let your requests be made known unto God. (7) And the peace of God, which passeth all understanding, shall keep your hearts and minds through Christ Jesus.

1 John 4:18

There is no fear in love, but perfect love casteth out fear; because fear hath torment. He that feareth is not made perfect in love.

Joshua 1:9

Have not I commanded thee? Be strong and of a good courage; be not afraid, neither be thou dismayed; for the Lord thy God is with thee whithersoever thou goest.

Psalms 34:4

I sought the Lord, and he heard me, and delivered me from all my fears.

Psalms 27:1

The Lord is my light and my salvation; whom shall I fear? The Lord is the strength of my life; of whom shall I be afraid?

Deuteronomy 31:6

Be strong and courageous. Do not be afraid or terrified because of them, for the Lord your God goes with you; he will never leave you nor forsake you.

Psalms 94:19 NIV

When anxiety was great within me, your consolation brought me joy.

Romans 8:38-39 (NIV)

For I am convinced that neither death nor life, neither angels nor demons, neither the present nor the future, nor any powers, (39) neither height nor depth, nor anything else in all creation, will be able to separate us from the love of God that is in Christ Jesus our Lord.

Matthew 6:34 NIV

Therefore do not worry about tomorrow, for tomorrow will worry about itself.   Each day has enough trouble of its own.

Psalms 32:7-8

Thou art my hiding place; thou shalt preserve me from trouble; thou shalt compass me about with songs of deliverance. Selah (8) I will instruct thee and teach thee in the way which thou shalt go: I will guide thee with mine eye.

I Peter 5:6 NIV

Humble yourselves, therefore, under God's mighty hand, that he may lift you up in due time.

Genesis 50:21

Now therefore fear ye not: I will nourish you, and your little ones. And he comforted them, and spake kindly unto them.

Romans 15:13

Now the God of hope fill you with all joy and peace in believing, that ye may abound in hope, through the power of the Holy Ghost.

Isaiah 35:4

Say to them that are of a fearful heart, Be strong, fear not: behold, your God will come with vengeance, even God with a recompense; he will come and save you.

Mark 6:50

For they all saw him, and were troubled. And immediately he talked with them, and saith unto them, "Be of good cheer: it is I; be not afraid."

Psalms 118:6-7

The Lord is on my side; I will not fear: what can man do unto me? (7) The Lord taketh my part with them that help me: therefore shall I see my desire upon them that hate me.

Revelation 1:17

And when I saw him, I fell at his feet as dead. And he laid his right hand upon me, saying unto me, "Fear not; I am the first and the last:"

Isaiah 43:1 NIV

But now, this is what the Lord says he who created you, Jacob, he who formed you Israel: "Do not fear, for I have redeemed you; I have summoned you by name; you are mine.

Psalms 115:11, 13

Ye that fear the Lord, trust in the Lord: he is their help and their shield. (13) He will bless them that fear the Lord, both small and great.

Section 6.1: *Your Notes on Fear*
List the Bible scriptures that best help you with your fears. Say them out loud throughout the day.

Section 7: Depression Scriptures

In the previous section, we talked about fear and a few reasons for fear. Because of the worldwide pandemic we mentioned, many had to be quarantined or we were under a lockdown in our homes for a while. You say it is no wonder so many were depressed during this time. But again, what does the Bible say about this?

Isaiah 40:31

But they that wait upon the Lord shall renew their strength; they shall mount up with wings as eagles; they shall run, and not be weary; and they shall walk, and not faint.

Proverbs 12:25

Heaviness in the heart of man maketh it stoop: but a good word maketh it glad.

I Peter 5:7

Casting all your care upon him; for he careth for you.

Jeremiah 29:11 (NIV)

For I know the plans I have for you, declares the Lord, plans to prosper you and not to harm you, plans to give you hope and a future.

Psalms 143:7

Hear me speedily, O Lord; my spirit faileth: hide not thy face from me, lest I be like unto them that go down into the pit.

Isaiah 41:10

Fear not; for I am with thee: be not dismayed; for I am thy God: I will strengthen thee; yea, I will help thee; yea, I will uphold thee with the right hand of my righteousness.

Psalms 34:17-18

The righteous cry out, and the Lord hears them; he delivers them from all their troubles. (18) The Lord is close to the brokenhearted and saves those who are crushed in spirit.

Romans 12:2

And be not conformed to this world: but be ye transformed by the renewing of your mind that ye may prove what is that good, and acceptable, and perfect will of God.

John 16:32 NIV

"A time is coming and in fact has come when you will be scattered, each to your own home. You will leave me all alone. Yet I am not alone, for my Father is with me.

Psalms 40:1-2

I waited patiently for the Lord; and he inclined unto me, and heard my cry. (2) He brought me up also out of a horrible pit, out of the miry clay, and set my feet upon a rock, and established my goings.

Psalms 30:11

Thou hast turned for me my mourning into dancing: thou hast put off my sackcloth, and girded me with gladness.

John 10:10

The thief cometh not, but for to steal, and to kill, and to destroy: I am come that they might have life, and that they might have it more abundantly.

Revelation 21:4

And God shall wipe away all tears from their eyes; and there shall be no more death, neither sorrow, nor crying, neither shall there be any more pain: for the former things are passed away.

I Timothy 4:12NIV

Don't let anyone look down on you because you are young, but set an example for the believers in speech, in conduct, in love, in faith and in purity.

Luke 12:25-27

Who of you by worrying can add a single hour to your life? (26) Since you cannot do this very little thing, why do you worry about the rest? (27) "Consider how the wild flowers grow. They do not labor or spin. Yet I tell you, not even Solomon in all his splendor was dressed like one of these".

Section 7.1: *Your Notes on Depression*

Write down some of the ways the Bible instructs us concerning our fears and anxieties.

Section 8: Healing & Sickness

The Bible speaks of physical and spiritual healing. Read the following scriptures to see which ones apply to your situation. It's always good to memorize a few of these just to keep in mind what the Bible is telling you at this time.

Proverbs 17:22

A merry heart doeth good like a medicine: but a broken spirit drieth the bones.

Philippians 4:19

But my God shall supply all your need according to his riches in glory by Christ Jesus.

Romans 5:3-4 NIV

Not only so, but we also glory in our sufferings, because we know that suffering produces perseverance; perseverance, character; and character, hope.

2 Chronicles 7:14

If my people, which are called by my name, shall humble themselves, and pray, and seek my face, and turn from their wicked ways; then I will hear from heaven, and will forgive their sin, and will heal their land.

Jeremiah 17:14

Heal me, O Lord, and I shall be healed; save me, and I shall be saved: for thou art my praise.

James 5:14-15

Is any sick among you? Let him call for the elders of the

church; and let them pray over him, anointing him with oil in the name of the Lord: (15) and the prayer of faith shall save the sick, and the Lord shall raise him up; and if he has committed sins, they shall be forgiven him.

Isaiah 53:4-5 NIV

Surly he took up our pain and bore our suffering, yet we considered him punished by God, stricken by him, and afflicted. (5) But he was pierced for our transgressions, he was crushed for our iniquities; the punishment that brought us peace was on him, and by his wounds we are healed.

James 5:16

Confess your faults one to another, and pray one for another, that ye may be healed. The effectual fervent prayer of a righteous man availeth much

Isaiah 57:18-19

I have seen his ways, and will heal him: I will lead him also, and restore comforts unto him and to his mourners. (19) I create the fruit of the lips; Peace, peace to him that is far off, and to him that is near, saith the Lord; and I will heal him.

Jeremiah 30:17

For I will restore health unto thee, and I will heal thee of thy wounds, saith the Lord; because they called thee an Outcast, saying, This is Zion, whom no man seeketh after.

Exodus 23:25

And ye shall serve the Lord your God, and he shall bless thy bread, and thy water; and I will take sickness away from the midst of thee.

Exodus 15:26

And said, If thou wilt diligently hearken to the voice of the Lord thy God, and wilt do that which is right in his sight, and wilt give ear to his commandments, and keep all his statues, I will put none of these diseases upon thee, which I brought upon the Egyptians: for I am the Lord that healeth thee.

Isaiah 38:16-17 NIV

Lord, by such things people live; and my spirit finds life in them too. You restored me to health and let me live. (17) Surly it was for my benefit that I suffered such anguish. In your love you kept me from the pit of destruction; you have put all my sins behind your back.

Deuteronomy 32:39 NIV

See now that I myself am he! There is no god besides me. I put to death and I bring to life, I have wounded and I will heal, and no one can deliver out of my hand.

Proverbs 4:20-22 NIV

My son, pay attention to what I say; turn your ear to my words. (21) Do not let them out of your sight, keep them within your heart; (22) for they are life to those who find them and health to one's whole body.

Psalms 107:19-21 NIV

Then they cried to the Lord in their trouble, and he saved them from their distress. (20) He sent out his word and healed them; he rescued them from the grave. (21) Let them give thanks to the Lord for his unfailing love and his wonderful deeds for mankind.

Ecclesiastes 23:1

To everything there is a season, and a time to every purpose under the heaven

Ecclesiastes 23:2-4

A time to be born, and a time to die; a time to plant, and a time to pluck up that which is planted; (3) A time to kill, and a time to heal; a time to break down, and a time to build up;(4) A time to weep, and a time to laugh; a time to mourn, and a time to dance;

Ecclesiastes 23:5-8

A time to cast away stones, and a time to gather stones together; a time to embrace, and a time to refrain from embracing; (6) A time to get, and a time to lose; a time to keep, and a time to cast away; (7) A time to rend, and a time to sew; a time to keep silence, and a time to speak; (8) A time to love, and a time to hate; a time of war, and a time of peace.

Section 8.1: *Healing & Sickness Notes*
List if you need physical or spiritual healing. Then list a few scriptures pertaining to your specific needs.

Section 9: Concerning Children

We all are children of God our Father. He loves us, instructs us. He even disciplines us. Therefore, God expects us to do the same to our children.

Ephesians 6:1-3

Children, obey your parents in the Lord: for this is right. (2) Honor thy father and mother; (which is the first commandment with promise;) (3) That it may be well with thee, and thou mayest live long on the earth.

Ephesians 6:4

And, ye fathers provoke not your children to wrath: but bring them up in the nurture and admonition of the Lord.

Deuteronomy 6:5-6

And thou shalt love the Lord thy God with all thine heart, and with all thy soul, and with all thy might. (6) And these words which I command thee this day, shall be in thine heart:

Deuteronomy 6:7

And thou shalt teach them diligently unto thy children, and shalt talk of them when thou sittest in thine house, and when thou walkest by the way, and when thou liest down, and when thou risest up.

Proverbs 22:6

Train up a child in the way he should go; and when he is old, he will not depart from it.

Psalms 139:14

I will praise thee; for I am fearfully and wonderfully made: marvelous are thy works; and that my soul knoweth right well.

Exodus 20:12

Honor thy father and thy mother: that thy days may be long upon the land which the Lord thy God giveth thee

Luke 18:16-17

But Jesus called unto him, and said, "Suffer little children to come unto me, and forbid them not: for of such is the kingdom of God. (17) Verily I say unto you, whosoever shall not receive the kingdom of God as a little child shall in no wise enter therein."

Proverbs 22:15

Foolishness is bound in the heart of a child, but the rod of correction shall drive it far from him.

Proverbs 29:15, 17

The rod and reproof give wisdom: but a child left to himself bringeth his mother to shame (17) Correct thy son, and he shall give thee rest; yea, he shall give delight unto thy soul.

Proverbs 20:11

Even a child is known by his doings, whether his work be pure, and whether it be right.

Titus 2:6, 7 (NIV)

Similarly, encourage the young men to be self-controlled. (7) In everything set them an example by doing what is good. In your teaching show integrity, seriousness and soundness of speech

Jeremiah 1:5

Before I formed thee in the belly, I knew thee; and before thou camest forth out of the womb I sanctified thee, and I ordained thee a prophet unto the nations.

Proverbs 23:13-14

Withhold not correction from the child: for if thou beatest him with the rod, he shall not die. (14) Thou shalt beat him with the rod, and shalt deliver his soul from hell.

Proverbs 1:8

My son, hear the instruction of thy father, and forsake not the law of thy mother:

Hebrews 12:11 (NIV)

No discipline seems pleasant at the time, but painful. Later on, however, it produces a harvest of righteousness and peace for those who have been trained by it.

III John 1:4 (NIV)

I have no greater joy than to hear that my children walk in truth.

Psalms 8:2

Out of the mouth of babes and sucklings hast thou ordained strength because of thine enemies, that thou mightiest still the enemy and the avenger.

Psalms 34:11

Come, ye children, hearken unto me: I will teach you the fear of the Lord.

Matthew 18:2-4

And Jesus called a little child unto him, and set him in the midst of them, (3) And said, "Verily I say unto you, except ye be converted, and become as little children, ye shall not enter into the kingdom of heaven. (4) Whosoever therefore shall humble himself as this little child, the same is greatest in the kingdom of heaven. (5) And whoso shall receive one such little child in my name receiveth me.

Matthew 18:10-14

Take heed that ye despise not one of these little ones; for I say unto you, That in heaven their angels do always behold the face of my Father which is in heaven. (11) For the Son of man is come to save that which was lost. (12) How think ye? If a man has a hundred sheep, and one of them be gone astray, doth he not leave the ninety and nine, and goeth into the mountains, and seeketh that which is gone astray?   (13) And if so be that he finds it, verily I say unto you, he rejoiceth more of that sheep, than of the ninety and nine which went not astray. (14) Even so it is not the will of your Father which is in heaven, that one of these little ones should perish.

Matthew 21:15-16

And when the chief priests and scribes saw the wonderful things that he did, and the children crying in the temple, and saying, Hosanna to the Son of David; they were sore displeased, (16) And said unto him, Hearest thou what these say? And Jesus saith unto them, "Yea, have ye never read, Out of the mouth of babes and sucklings thou hast perfected praise?"

Psalms 127:3-5

Lo, children are an heritage of the Lord: and the fruit of the womb is his reward. (4) As arrows are in the hand of a mighty man; so are children of the youth. (5) Happy is the man that hath his quiver full of them: they shall not be ashamed, but they shall speak with the enemies in the gate.

II Timothy 3:14-15

But continue thou in the things which thou hast learned and hast been assured of, knowing of whom thou hast learned them; (15) And that from a child thou hast known the holy scriptures, which are ble to make thee wise unto salvation through faith which is in Christ Jesus.

Section 9.1: *Notes Concerning Children*

Write down a few examples of how God instructs us concerning children. List where you feel you need to improve.

Section 10: Scriptures to Feed On

The following pages are just a few scriptures to feed on and to study. It is still best to open your Bible and meditate on what the Lord has to say.

<u>II Timothy 2:15</u>

<u>Study to shew thyself approved unto God, a workman that needeth not to be ashamed, rightly dividing the word of truth.</u>

<u>Matthew 6:33</u>

But seek ye first the kingdom of God, and his righteousness; and all these things shall be added unto you.

<u>Proverbs 29:18</u>

 Where there is no vision, the people perish: but he that keepeth the law, happy is he.

<u>Habakkuk 2:2</u>

And the Lord answered me, and said, Write the vision, and make it plain upon tables, that he may run that readeth it.

<u>Romans 8:24-25NIV</u>

For in this we were saved. But hope that is seen is no hope at all. Who hopes for what they already have? (25) But if we hope for what we do not yet have, we wait for it patiently.

<u>Psalms 46:10</u>

He says, "Be still, and know that I am God; I will be

Proverbs 15:1

A soft answer turneth away wrath: but grievous words stir up anger.

John 15:7

If ye abide in me, and my words abide in you, ye shall ask what ye will, and it shall be done unto you. exalted among the nations, I will be exalted in the earth."

Isaiah 26:3

Thou will keep him in perfect peace, whose mind is stayed on thee, because he trusteth in thee.

Romans 6:23

For the wages of sin is death; but the gift of God is eternal life through Jesus Christ our Lord.

II Peter 3:18

But grow in grace, and in the knowledge of our Lord and Saviour Jesus Christ. To him be glory both now and forever. Amen

Matthew 4:19

And he saith unto them, Follow me, and I will make you fishers of men.

John 14:18

I will not leave you comfortless: I will come to you.

Joshua 1:8

This book of the law shall not depart out of thy mouth; but thou shalt meditate therein day and night, that thou mayest observe to do according to all that is written therein: for then thou shalt make thy way prosperous, and then thou shalt have good success.

I John 2:1

My little children, these things write I unto you, that ye sin not. And if any man sin, we have an advocate with the Father, Jesus Christ the righteous;

I John 2:15-16

Love not the world, neither the things that are in the world. If any man love the world, the love of the Father is not in him. (16) For all that is in the world, the lust of the flesh, and the lust of the eyes, and the pride of life,

is not of the Father, but is of the world.

Proverbs 18:21

Death and life are in the power of the tongue: and they that love it shall eat the fruit thereof.

Hebrews 4:12

For the word of God is quick, and powerful, and sharper than any two-edged sword, piercing even to the dividing asunder of soul and spirit, and of the joints and marrow, and is a discerner of the thoughts and intents of the heart.

Matthew 25:40

And the King shall answer and say unto them, Verily I say unto you, In as much as ye have done it unto one of the least of these my brethren, ye have done it unto me.

Luke 16:10

He that is faithful in that which is least is faithful also in much: and he that is unjust in the least is unjust also in much.

Galatians 5:22, 23

But the fruit of the Spirit is love, joy, peace, longsuffering, gentleness, faith, (23) Meekness, temperance: against such there is no law.

John 3:16

For God so loved the world, that he gave his only begotten Son, that whosoever believeth in him should not perish, but have everlasting life.

John 3:17

For God sent not his Son into the world to condemn the world; but that the world through him might be saved.

John 3:18

He that believeth on him is not condemned: but he that believeth not is condemned already, because he hath not believed in the name of the only begotten Son of God.

Romans 10:9

That if thou shalt confess with thy mouth the Lord Jesus, and shalt believe in thine heart that God hath raised him from the dead, thou shalt be saved.

John 8:36

So if the Son sets you free, you will be free indeed.

Philippians 4:8

Finally, brethren, whatsoever things are true, whatsoever things are honest, whatsoever things are just, whatsoever things are pure, whatsoever things are lovely, whatsoever things are of good report; if there be any virtue, and if there be any praise, think on these things.

Proverbs 16:18

Pride goeth before destruction, and a haughty spirit before a fall.

Isaiah 43:2 (NIV)

When thou pass through the waters, I will be with you; and when you pass through the rivers, they will not sweep over you. When you walk through the fire, you will not be burned; the flames will not set you ablaze.

John 14:6

Jesus saith unto him, I am the way, the truth, and the life: no man cometh unto the Father, but by me.

Hebrews 10:23

Let us hold fast the profession of our faith without wavering (for he is faithful that promised)

St. John 1:12

But as many as received him, to them gave he power to become the sons of God, even to them that believe on his name:

Acts 1:8

But ye shall receive power, after that the Holy Ghost is come upon you: and ye shall be witnesses unto me both in Jerusalem, and in Judea, and in Samaria, and unto the uttermost part of the earth.

St. John 14:1

Let not your heart be troubled; ye believe in God, believe also in me.

James 2:26

For as the body without the spirit is dead, so faith without works is dead.

I Corinthians 6:19-20

What? Know ye not that your body is the temple of the Holy Ghost which is in you, which ye have of God, and ye are not your own? (20) For ye are bought with a price; therefore, glorify God in your body, and in your spirit, which are God's.

II Corinthians 5:17

Therefore, if any man be in Christ, he is a new creature; old things are passed away; behold, all things are become new.

I Timothy 2:5

For there is one God, and one mediator between God and men, the man Christ Jesus;

I Corinthians 10:13

There hath no temptation taken you but such as is common to man; but God is faithful, who will not suffer you to be tempted above that ye are able; but will with the temptation also make a way to escape, that ye may be able to bear it.

Galatians 2:20

I am crucified with Christ; nevertheless I live; yet not I, but Christ liveth in me; and the life which I now live in the flesh I live by the faith of the Son of God, who loved me, and gave himself for me.

Isaiah 53:6

All we like sheep have gone astray; we have turned everyone to his own way; and the Lord hath laid on him the iniquity of us all.

Joshua 24:15

And if it seems evil unto you to serve the Lord, choose you this day whom ye will serve; whether the gods which your fathers served that were on the other side of the flood, or the gods of the Amorites, in whose land ye dwell: but for me and my house, we will serve the Lord.

Malachi 3:10

Bring ye all the tithes into the storehouse, that there

may be meat in mine house, and prove me now herewith, saith the Lord of hosts, if I will not open you the windows of heaven, and pour you out a blessing, that there shall not be room enough to receive it.

Luke 19:10

For the Son of man is come to seek and to save and to save that which was lost.

John 17:17

Sanctify them through thy truth: thy word is truth.

Matthew 18:20

"For where two or three are gathered together in my name, there am I in the midst of them.

I Corinthians 15:58

Therefore, my beloved brethren, be ye steadfast, unmovable, always abounding in the work of the Lord, forasmuch as ye know that your labor is not in vain in the Lord.

Romans 12: 1

I beseech you therefore, brethren, by the mercies of God, that ye present your bodies a living sacrifice, holy, acceptable unto God, which is your reasonable service.

John 5:24

Verily, verily, I say unto you, He that heareth my word, and believeth on him that sent me, hath everlasting life, and shall not come into condemnation; but is passed from death unto life.

Psalms 122:1

I was glad when they said unto me, Let us go into the house of the Lord.

Psalms 121:1,2

I will lift up mine eyes unto the hills, from whence cometh my help. (2) My help cometh from the Lord, which made heaven and earth.

Revelation 3:20

Behold, I stand at the door, and knock: if any man hear my voice, and open the door, I will come in to him, and will sup with him, and he with me.

Psalms 119:105

Thy word is a lamp unto my feet, and a light unto my path.

James 1:22

But be ye doers of the word, and not hearers only, deceiving your own selves.

I Thessalonians 5:17, 18

Pray without ceasing. (18) In everything give thanks: for this is the will of God in Christ Jesus concerning you.

Colossians 4:6

Let your speech be always with grace, seasoned with salt, that ye may know how ye ought to answer every man.

Philippians 2:5

Let this mind be in you, which was also in Christ Jesus:

James 4:7-8

Submit yourselves therefore to God. Resist the devil, and he will flee from you. (8) Draw nigh to God, and he will draw nigh to you. Cleanse your hands, ye sinners; and purify your hearts, ye double-minded.

James 4:17

Therefore, to him that knoweth to do good, and doeth it not, to him it is sin.

Mark 8:36

For what shall it profit a man, if he shall gain the whole world, and lose his soul?

Psalms 119:11

Thy word have I hidden in mine heart, that I might not sin against thee.

II Timothy 3:16

All scripture is given by inspiration of God, and is profitable for doctrine, for reproof, for correction, for instruction in righteousness:

Luke 6:38 (NIV)

Give, and it will be given to you. A good measure, pressed down, shaken together and running over, will be poured into your lap. For with the measure you use, it will be measured to you.

Ephesians 6:11

Put on the whole armor of God that ye may be able to stand against the wiles of the devil.

Psalms 107:1

O give thanks unto the Lord, for he is good; for his mercy endureth forever.

Luke 6:49(NIV)

But the one who hears my words and does not put them into practice is like a man who built a house on the ground without a foundation. The moment the torrent struck that house, it collapsed and its destruction was complete.

Psalms 91:1,2

He who dwelleth in the secret place of the Most High shall abide under the shadow of the Almighty. (2) I will say of the Lord, He is my refuge and my fortress, my God; in him will I trust.

Matthew 6:9-13

The Lord's Prayer

Our Father which art in heaven, Hallowed be thy name. Thy kingdom come. Thy will be done in earth, as it is in heaven. Give us this day our daily bread. And forgive us our debts, as we forgive our debtors. And lead us not into temptation, but deliver us from evil: For thine is the kingdom, and the power, and the glory, forever. Amen

Psalms 150:6

Let everything that hath breath praise the Lord. Praise ye the Lord.

Daniel 10:2-3

The Daniel Fast

At that time I, Daniel, mourned for three weeks. I ate no choice food; no meat or wine touched my lips; and I used no lotions at all until the three weeks were over.

Psalms 23:1-6

A Psalm of David

The Lord is my shepherd; I shall not want. He maketh me to lie down in green pastures; he leadeth me beside the still waters. He restoreth my soul: he leadeth me in the paths of righteousness for his name sake. Yea, though I walk through the valley of the shadow of death, I will fear no evil: for thou art with me; thy rod and thy staff they comfort me. Thou prepareth a table before me in the presence of mine enemies; thou anointest my head with oil; my cup runneth over. Surely goodness and mercy shall follow me all the days of my life: and I will dwell in the house of the Lord forever.

Luke 6:12-16

The Twelve Disciples Chosen

And it came to pass in those days, that he went out into a mountain to pray, and continued all night in prayer to God. (13) And when it was day, he called unto him his disciples; and of them he chose twelve, whom also he named apostles; (14) Simon, (whom he also named Peter,) and Andrew his brother, James and John, Philip and Bartholomew, (15) Matthew and Thomas, James the *son* of Alphaeus, and Simon called Zelotes, (16) And Judas *the brother* of James, and Judas Iscariot, which also was the traitor,

Matthew 5:1-12

The Beatitudes

And seeing the multitudes, he went up into a mountain; and when he was set his disciples came unto him: (2) and he opened his mouth, and taught them, saying, (3) Blessed are the poor in spirit; for theirs is the kingdom of heaven. (4) Blessed are they that mourn; for they shall be comforted. (5) Blessed are the meek; for they shall inherit the earth. (6) Blessed are they which do hunger and thirst after righteousness; for they shall be filled. (7) Blessed are the merciful; for they shall obtain mercy. (8) Blessed are the pure in heart; for they shall see God. (9) Blessed are the peacemakers; for they shall be called the children of God. (10) Blessed are they which are persecuted for righteousness' sake; for theirs is the kingdom of heaven. (11) Blessed are ye, when men shall revile you, and persecute you, and shall say all manner of evil against you falsely, for my sake. (12) Rejoice, and be exceeding glad; for great is your reward in heaven; for so persecuted they the prophets which were before you.

Section 10.1: General Notes

List scriptures that you want to read more of what the Bible says about it.

____
____
____
____
____
____
____
____
____
____
____
____
____
____
____
____
____
____
____
____
____

Section 11: Old Testament Names

Genesis	Ecclesiastes
Exodus	Song of Solomon
Leviticus	Isaiah
Numbers	Jeremiah
Deuteronomy	Lamentation
Joshua	Ezekiel
Judges	Daniel
Ruth	Hosea
I Samuel	Joel
II Samuel	Amos
I Kings	Obadiah
II Kings	Jonah
I Chronicles	Micah
II Chronicles	Nahum
Ezra	Habakkuk
Nehemiah	Zephaniah
Esther	Haggai
Job	Zechariah
Psalms	Malachi
Proverbs	

Section 12: New Testament Names

Matthew	I Timothy
Mark	II Timothy
Luke	Titus
John	Philemon
The Acts	Hebrews
Romans	James
I Corinthians	I Peter
II Corinthians	II Peter
Galatians	I John
Ephesians	II John
Philippians	III John
Colossian	Jude
I Thessalonians	Revelation
II Thessalonians	

Study to Shew Thyself Approved